Head of Blind-worm. 1/2

A Book-scorpion (*Chelifer cancroides*). 5/1

a Cotton-stainer

Epeiridæ.
a, male, and *b*, female, of *Epeira stellata*; *c*, characteristic orb-web of an epeirid (*Epeira strix*).

The Dr Dragon (*Drac eatus*).

Proxys punctulatus.

Click-beetle, natural size.

a
Hellgrammite (*a*) and Hellgrammite-fly.

Parasite of the Beaver (*Platypsylius castoris*). (Line shows natural size.)

Agonoderus dorsalis (Le Conte). Vertical line shows natural size.

Hawthorn-tingis (*arcuata*), one of the enlarged about ten tim

The Twig-girdler (*Oncideres cingulata*). 1/1
a, a branch girdled by the beetle.

Sinea diadema, one of the *Reduviidæ*. (Line shows natural size.)

The Bait-bug.

Rose-beetle (*Cetonia aurata*). Vertical line shows natural size.

-beetle (*Ten* (Line show

Galeruca notata

bee

be

by

Ting Morris

illustrated by

Desiderio Sanzi

designed by

Deb Miner

A⁺

SMART APPLE MEDIA

You are in a patch of clover, where brightly colored flowers grow. Lots of busy bees are buzzing about.

Watch them land on the sweet-smelling clover. See them fly in and out of the flowers. Count them coming and going. What are they doing, and where do they live?

Turn the page and take a closer look.

The bees' nest is in this hollow tree trunk. It is the home of a colony of wild honey-bees, and on this warm summer's day, there is a stream of busy workers flying in and out.

If you ever spot a bees' nest, don't get too close. Bees get very angry if their home is disturbed and will sting to defend themselves.

THE NEST

Wild honeybees usually make their nests in rock caves or hollow trees. Some nests house up to 60,000 bees. Inside the nest, the bees build wax combs. The combs are upright sheets covered on both sides with thousands of tiny rooms called wax cells.

RENT A NEST

Bumblebees are different from honey-bees. They make their nests underground, sometimes in an old mouse nest. Only 20 to 150 bees live in a bumblebee nest.

WAX-WORKERS

Worker bees make the wax in their glands, and it comes out through small holes in their bodies. They pick off the tiny white flakes of wax with their legs, chew them, and put the wax on the walls of the cells they are building.

NO WASTE OF SPACE

Each cell has six sides, and all of the cells fit together perfectly. In some cells, the bees raise their growing young. In others, they store honey and pollen. The cell walls are tilted so that the honey can't run out.

A WORKER BEE'S BODY

A bee's body has three parts—the HEAD, the chest (called the THORAX), and the ABDOMEN, which includes a honey stomach. A bee carries nectar in its honey stomach. A bee's whole body is covered with furry hairs. The black and yellow stripes are warning colors.

A bee has five EYES: a big one on each side of its head, and three small ones on top.

Bees pick up smells with their FEELERS (called antennae).

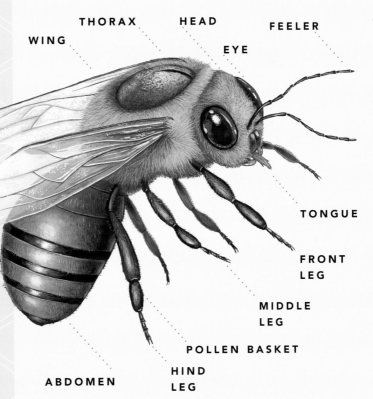

WING   THORAX   HEAD   FEELER   EYE

The TONGUE is a long tube used to suck up water, nectar, and honey. Bees hold wax and pollen with their jaws.

TONGUE
FRONT LEG
MIDDLE LEG
POLLEN BASKET
HIND LEG
ABDOMEN

With its two pairs of WINGS, a bee can fly forward, backward, and sideways, as well as hover in the air.

A bee uses the combs on its back LEGS to scrape pollen into special POLLEN BASKETS on the outside of its back legs.

There's no relaxing in the sunshine for these workers. **They are the field bees in charge of finding and collecting food for the colony.** They fly out to flowers and bring back pollen and nectar.

The guards at the nest entrance know every bee in the nest and keep out unwelcome strangers. They kill enemies with their stingers. Look at the bee loaded with yellow pollen. She has good news. There's a patch of sweet clover and foxgloves nearby!

WHO LIVES IN THE COLONY?

Honeybees are social insects. They live in large family groups and all share in the work.

THE QUEEN She is the biggest bee and does nothing but stay at home and lay eggs. The queen is the mother of all the bees in the nest.

STINGER WARNING!

A worker bee has a barbed, poisonous stinger. If it digs into an enemy, the bee will die because the barbs hold tight and rip out its abdomen. But the queen can sting a number of times because she has a smooth, curved stinger.

SMELLS RIGHT

All of the bees in a nest have the same smell, because they all eat the same food. If a bee with the wrong smell tries to get in, the guards drive her away. There are many animals that would like to steal their honey.

WORKERS They are smaller female bees who serve the queen. Field bees collect food for the colony, and house bees work in the nest.

DRONES They are the male bees. Their only job is to fertilize the queen during her mating flight.

Dance, dance! Show us where the flowers grow!

The other bees in the nest can smell sweet nectar on their sister. She is dancing round and round on the comb to tell her nest-mates where she found clover and flowers. She is going faster and faster. Now the bees know that there's lots of food close to the nest. They join in the dance and learn the way to the clover patch.

MAKING A BEELINE

When a field worker finds flowers, she makes a beeline for the nest by flying straight there. Her smell tells the other bees which flowers to look for.

WAGGLE DANCE

If the food is far away, the bee waggles her abdomen and dances up and down inside the nest. She turns left and right to make a figure-eight and shows the distance to the food by the length of the straight runs and the number of waggles. The faster she waggles, the more nectar there is. Bees find the flowers by the sun. A straight run upward means that the food is toward the sun. A straight run downward means that it's away from the sun.

ROUND DANCE

If the food is near the nest, the field bee dances in circles. She moves around clockwise and counterclockwise on the combs. The faster she dances, the more flowers there are. The other bees follow her steps, and by copying her movements they learn the way to the flowers.

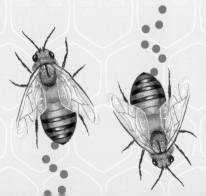

11

FLOWER POWER

Flowers attract insects with their sweet smell and bright colors. They do this because they need bees and other insects to carry pollen grains, which are made by a flower's male parts, to the eggs made by the female parts. Bees visit different flowers and mix the pollen and the eggs. This process is called pollination, and it helps plants to make seeds that grow into other plants.

Once they are sure of the way, hundreds of field bees zoom off to the clover patch. **The best time to get nectar is when the sun is high and the flowers are fully open.** The flight path is busy, with honeybees buzzing back and forth. A message from the nest calls for extra supplies of poppy pollen. That means there's no rest for the field workers!

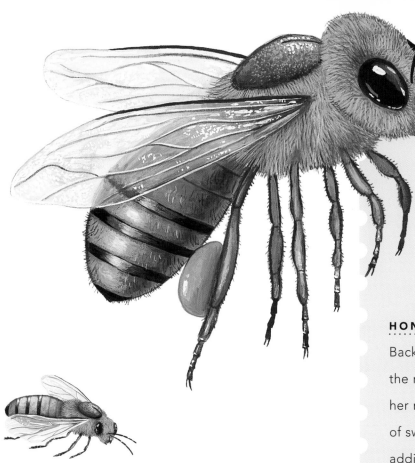

SWEET NECTAR

Nectar is a sweet, sugary liquid in flower blossoms. Bees suck it up, and during the flight home they store it inside their bodies in a pouch called a honey stomach.

HONEY, HONEY

Back in the nest, the field bee brings up the nectar, and a house bee sucks it from her mouth. The house bee chews the blob of sweet liquid for about 20 minutes, adding enzymes (chemicals that change the nectar). She stores the fluid in open cells and chews it again after a while. In the warm nest, the nectar dries out and turns into honey. Three days later, the house bee packs the honey into cells and seals them with a cap of wax. Honey is the bees' food supply.

HONEYCOMB

Combs with cells full of honey are called honeycombs. You can buy pieces of honeycomb—they taste delicious!

BAG LADIES

Field bees collect pollen and nectar. Pollen is the fine, powdery dust in flowers. It gets caught on the bee's hairy body when she walks over the flowers to suck the nectar. She combs the grains into the pollen bags on her back legs. Pollen is an important food source for young, growing bees.

Inside the nest, the queen bee is served by her ladies-in-waiting. She has just let them know that she's taken a liking to some poppy pollen. She wants more for herself and the grubs. This information is passed on from nurse bees to house bees and finally to the field bees.

The bees have a lot of work to do, because the queen is laying more than 1,000 eggs a day. Cells have to be cleaned, new cells have to be built, and more honey has to be made.

BUSY TONGUES

Messages get around the whole colony because bees share food all the time. They pass nectar to each other through their tongues.

ROYAL MESSAGE

The queen bee makes special chemicals in glands around her mouth to pass information on to other bees. Her ladies-in-waiting lick these liquid messages when they feed the queen.

WORK SCHEDULES

In the summer, a worker bee lives only for about six weeks. During that time she takes on different duties.

WEEK 1 First she is a cleaner, preparing cells for new eggs. After three days, she becomes a nurse, feeding pollen and honey to the grubs.

WEEK 2 By the sixth day, she becomes a lady-in-waiting. She feeds the queen and the larvae with royal jelly. She does this job for about a week. Then she becomes a builder of wax cells.

WEEKS 3-6 Around the 16th day, she becomes a storeroom attendant. She takes in nectar and pollen from the field bees, spending her time turning the nectar into honey. On about the 20th day, she stands guard at the nest entrance. From the third week until the end of her life, she is a field bee on food duty.

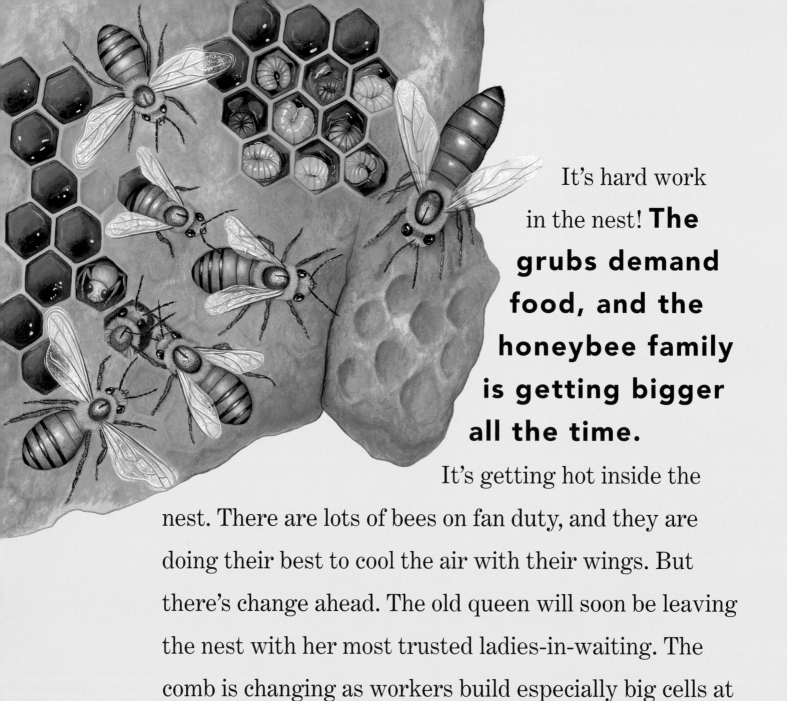

It's hard work in the nest! **The grubs demand food, and the honeybee family is getting bigger all the time.**

It's getting hot inside the nest. There are lots of bees on fan duty, and they are doing their best to cool the air with their wings. But there's change ahead. The old queen will soon be leaving the nest with her most trusted ladies-in-waiting. The comb is changing as workers build especially big cells at the edge. New queens will grow inside these cells.

QUEEN CELLS

Queen cells are bigger than worker cells. Royal grubs are fed only royal jelly. After 16 days, a big baby queen emerges.

ROYAL JELLY

This creamy food is full of vitamins. It comes from special glands in the heads of nurse bees. The queen bee and queen grubs live on it.

FROM EGG TO BEE

When a queen has mated with a male bee (called a drone), she can lay eggs for the rest of her life. The queen has ruled this nest for three years.

The queen lays one egg inside each cell.

After three days, the egg hatches into a larva, or grub. For the first three days, all of the grubs are fed royal jelly by nurse bees.

Nurse bees feed the grubs bee bread, a mixture of honey and pollen.

After five days, the nurses seal the cells with wax lids.

Inside its wax cell, each grub becomes a pupa and spins a covering of silk called a cocoon.

Gradually the grub takes on color.

A baby worker bee chews its way out of its wax cell 21 days after the egg was laid.

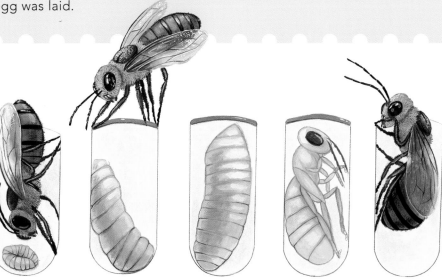

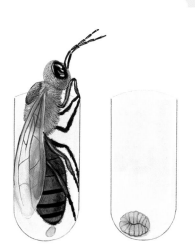

17

NEST-HUNTING

Scout bees dance on the swarm to get other scouts to look at possible nesting places. They check out each other's finds. After much buzzing about, they decide on a place and move in to start a new colony.

A queen knows when it's time to leave the old nest. Soon there will be no room for her in this crowded colony. She knows that her workers are feeding young queens, and her trusted servants are ready for the journey. They have filled themselves with honey and are waiting for her outside the nest. **Together they fly off to a nearby tree.** The swarm settles on a branch while scouts search for a new nesting site. When a scout finds a good place, she dances to show the others where it is.

SWARMING

The bees' flight to start a new colony is called swarming. This usually happens when the nest gets too full or when the queen is too old to lay enough eggs. The workers then build big cells for new queens to grow in. Just before the young queens are ready, the old queen gives the signal to leave. About half of the workers gather outside the nest and wait for their queen to come out. They cluster around her and fly up into the air.

19

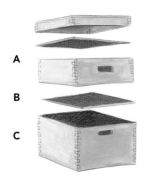

A MODERN BEEHIVE

Modern hives are wooden boxes with several drawer-like frames, called supers, that can be taken out. The bees build their combs in these frames. The lower section (**C**) is for the queen. The upper section (**A**) is for storing honey. The worker bees can get to all parts of the hive, but the queen is too big to get through the grid (**B**) into the honeycomb. She can lay her eggs only in the cells at the bottom.

20

What an amazing find! A wooden box with a sturdy roof, and inside is a place for honeycombs waiting to be filled. The queen starts laying eggs at once. Soon the house bees are busy building and cleaning, while field bees bring pollen and nectar from sunflowers nearby. The bees don't know that the hive was built by a beekeeper who will take away their honeycombs. But they are happy workers and make as much honey as they can.

HANDLE WITH CARE

When the beekeeper takes out the honeycombs, she must be careful not to get stung. She wears a wire screen to protect her face, and special clothes and gloves.

LONG AGO

People have been taking honey from bees for thousands of years. The first beekeepers put straw baskets, called skeps, near their homes. Bees flew inside and built their combs on sticks.

HONEYBEE SETTLERS

About 400 years ago, people from England took honeybees with them to America. Today's beekeepers look after millions of hives. Each year they produce about 200 million pounds (91 million kg) of honey. For every pound (450 g) of honey, bees collect nectar from more than two million flowers.

The old queen has gone.
Long live the new queen!
For a week, the young queen
has been eating lots of honey
to make her strong. She has killed her
rivals in their cells, and now the throne is hers.
Today she is going on her wedding flight. Look how she flies up
into the sky. Lots of drones chase her. The
young queen will choose
the one that can
fly the highest.

THE STRONGEST WINS

The first queen to emerge from her cell kills the others in their cells. If two queens come out at the same time, they fight until one is stung to death.

A BEE WEDDING

When the young queen is about a week old, she goes on her one and only wedding flight. She flies up into the sky, followed by lots of male drones. When a drone reaches her, he puts sperm into her body so she can make baby bees. After her wedding flight, the young queen flies back to rule her nest. The chosen drone dies soon after mating.

UNLUCKY DRONES

The other drones that don't mate with the queen go back to the nest and are fed by their sisters until fall. Then they are thrown out and die. Male bees can't feed themselves because their tongues are too short to get nectar.

SPRING EGGS

In spring, the honeybee queen
starts laying eggs again. The workers
clean out old cells and build new
ones for the growing grubs.

24

In wintertime, it's too cold for the honeybees to leave their nest. All the flowers have died, but the bees have stored enough honey to see them through the winter.

Inside the nest, they huddle together and shake their wings to stay warm.

Perhaps the bees are dreaming of sunny days, beautiful flowers, sweet nectar, and yellow pollen. When the first flowers open in spring, these honeybees will be buzzing about again.

25

The queen lays one egg
inside each wax cell.

Bee

The queen mates
with a drone.

Honeybees share
work in the colony.

Nurse bees feed the
grubs inside the cells.

Nurse bees seal the
cells with wax lids.

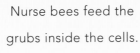

CIRCLE OF LIFE

The young bees emerge
from their cocoons.

barbed Pointy and angled; a barb is the part of a bee's stinger that acts like a hook.

cocoon A silky case spun by insect larvae, which protects them while they grow into pupae.

glands Organs in an animal's body that produce important substances.

grubs The young form of some insects; another word for larvae.

hive An artificial nesting box for bees, from which beekeepers can collect honey.

hover To stay in one place in the air.

nectar A sweet, sugary liquid produced by flowers.

nurse bees Bees that look after and feed baby bees.

pollen Powdery, dust-like grains made by flowers.

pollination The process by which a plant's pollen is mixed with eggs to make seeds and new plants.

queen A large female bee that lays eggs; there is one queen in every nest.

royal jelly A substance produced by worker bees that is used especially to feed the larvae that will become future queen bees.

sperm Fluid produced by male animals that makes a female's eggs grow into babies.

vitamins Substances found in food that are needed by animals for good health.

wedding flight A flight made by queen bees when they mate with male bees.

Published by Smart Apple Media

1980 Lookout Drive

North Mankato, Minnesota 56003

Illustration: Desiderio Sanzi

Design: Deb Miner

Library of Congress

Cataloging-in-Publication Data

Morris, Ting.

Bee / by Ting Morris.

p. cm. — (Creepy crawly world)

Summary: An introduction to the physical

characteristics, behavior, and life cycle

of bees.

ISBN 1-58340-378-7

1. Bees—Juvenile literature.

[1. Bees.] I. Title.

QL565.2.M685 2003

595.79'9—dc21 2002042815

Head of Blind-worm. $\frac{1}{2}$

Cotton-stainer
a, *b*

Epeiridæ.
a, male, and *b*, female, of *Epeira stellata*; *c*, characteristic orb-web of an epeirid (*Epeira strix*).

The Dr
Drago
(*Drac
eatus*)

A Book-scorpion (*Chelifer cancroides*). $\frac{5}{1}$

Proxys punctulatus.

Agonoderus dorsalis (Le Conte). Vertical line shows natural size.

Hawthorn-tingis *arcuata*), one of the enlarged about ten ti

Click-beetle, natural size.

Hellgrammite (*a*) and Hellgrammite-fly.

Parasite of the Beaver (*Platypsyllus castoris*). (Line shows natural size.)

The Twig-girdler (*Oncideres cingulata*). $\frac{1}{1}$
a, a branch girdled by the beetle.

Sinea diadema, one of the *Reduviidæ*. (Line shows natural size.)

The Bait-bug.

Rose-beetle (*Cetonia aurata*). Vertical line shows natural size.

Flour-beetle (*Te
litor*). (Line show
size.)

Galeruca notata

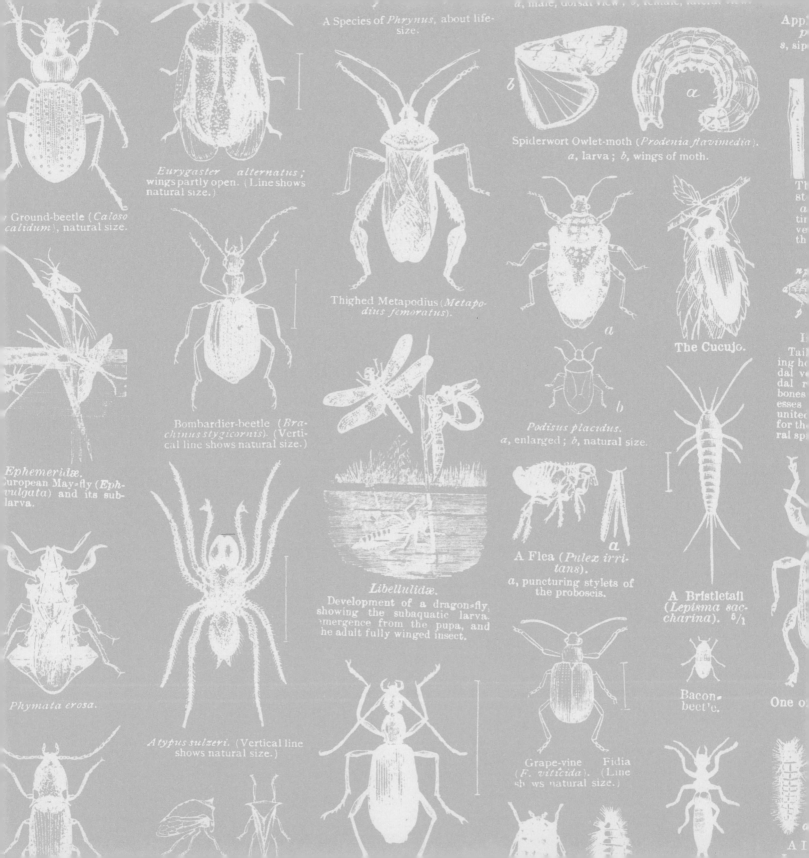

A Species of *Phrynus*, about life-size.

Eurygaster alternatus; wings partly open. (Line shows natural size.)

Ground-beetle (*Caloso calidum*), natural size.

Spiderwort Owlet-moth (*Prodenia flavimedia*). *a*, larva ; *b*, wings of moth.

Thighed Metapodius (*Metapodius femoratus*).

The Cucujo.

Ephemeridæ. European May-fly (*Eph-vulgata*) and its sub-larva.

Bombardier-beetle (*Bra-chinus stygicornis*). (Verti-cal line shows natural size.)

Podisus placidus. *a*, enlarged ; *b*, natural size.

Libellulidæ. Development of a dragon-fly, showing the subaquatic larva, emergence from the pupa, and the adult fully winged insect.

A Flea (*Pulex irri-tans*). *a*, puncturing stylets of the proboscis.

A Bristletail (*Lepisma sac-charina*). ⁵/₁

Phymata erosa.

Atypus sulzeri. (Vertical line shows natural size.)

Grape-vine Fidia (*F. viticida*). (Line shows natural size.)

Bacon-beet'e.

One o